The Nature of It All

Ryanna Hammond

Copyright © 2025 All With Heart

All rights reserved.

No part of this publication may be reproduced, distributed, or transmitted in any form. This includes photocopying, recording, or any electronic or mechanical methods, without the prior written permission of the author, except in the case of brief quotations embodied in critical reviews and certain other noncommercial uses permitted by copyright law.

Printed in the United States of America.

First paperback edition 2025

Cover design by Ryanna Hammond

ISBN-13: 979-8-218-63213-7

The Nature of It All

Ryanna Hammond

All titles by Ryanna Hammond

We Are Human
Hearts Bruise Never Break
My Cup of Coffee
The Door Between Us
Skinny Dipping with Patience
Searching For Emiliano

Ryanna Hammond's work appears in

Just Another Minute: Collection of Short Stories by Free Spirit
The Phoenix: Issue 58 by Pfeiffer University
California's Best Emerging Poets compiled by Z Publishing House
dialogue: reflection literary magazine by Empower Her* Voice's
(w)holes: An Anthology from the Heartland Society of Women Writers
and more appearances are sure to come!

Dedicated to Mother Nature

for helping me find my way home

"I like it when a flower or a little tuft of grass grows through a crack in the concrete. It's so fuckin' heroic."

– George Carlin

Content

Preface

a long-drawn sidewalk   15

cracks in the concrete   33

soil and a thicket   47

Other Works   73

Preface

It is fervently believed (thanks to various religions) that heaven and hell are our two potential destinations after death; some people, however, proudly argue that these places are fallacies born from scare tactics. Once in a blue moon, you might stumble across someone who shares my beliefs: (1) We need not fret or guess about the potential of the afterlife because where we are now is alive on Earth. (2) Heaven and hell are two opposing ends of a wide spectrum of Consciousness in the here and now on Earth. In other words, "heaven on earth" is not a phrase signifying an ideal dream — it is a state of being that we can tap into or reside in when we are living soulfully from Peace and Love. Hell on earth, then, is a state where one's reality is riddled with anxiety, chaos, self-hate, victimhood, and/or a disconnection from our Source. Just like anything in life, there exists a gray area comprised of elements of both heaven and hell. Where we exist on the spectrum is closely related to our level of self-awareness and our daily choices and decisions. While we don't have control over everything that happens in our lives, we do have control over ourselves. Thus, scary as it may be to hear, where we exist on this earnest spectrum is entirely up to us. We choose to stay or leave a terrible job. We choose to stay or leave toxic relationships. We choose to learn from or ignore our life lessons. We choose to speak up or stay quiet. We choose to follow our intuition or stay trapped in societal boxes and chains of others' expectations.

So, why am I sharing this? Because I have lived in hell. In fact, I've looked the devil in the eyes quite a few times. This is my journey out of the flames. This is my journey to heaven.

With love,
Ryanna Hammond

Instagram: @soulledwanderess
TikTok: @soulledwanderess

A LONG-DRAWN SIDEWALK

THE NATURE OF IT ALL

a compilation of excuses

happy couples are everywhere
on instagram / i eagerly post a picture
of my boyfriend and i / he asks why
i felt the need to post it / i didn't
like how that made me feel and asked
when he'll post one of us / once a week
he tells me another reason he hasn't /
i've compiled the unbelievable list like
grocery items that don't exist /
he doesn't want to flex / he doesn't
want men clicking on my profile /
people have stalked him / once
he gets his car working he will /
he likes his privacy / he's scared
in case we break up / apparently i don't understand
poverty / we don't have enough
pictures together / the photos he liked
got deleted / it's cool
to not post / he will
post about us when he's proud / he isn't
sure what to post / he wants to
stay true to himself / he doesn't
like his face / only girls
post a bunch / there's more important things to do /
he *wants* to post one / he just doesn't
like posting /

RYANNA HAMMOND

Seven Deadly Serpents

    the serpents knew my weakness: a ripe, crisp ap-
     pealing man who wouldn't know how to love me.
        one glance and i became a salacious girl, lost
            a chamber of my heart to lust. grew hungry,
                licked the hypnotizing man's skin. he tasted
                    tangy and sweet. i wanted—no, needed—
                  more and more and more, lost my sense
                of taste to gluttony for over-indulging in
                my man's yellow–brown speckled eyes,
                that were more alluring than time
                alone in nature. i stomached an ache
            from the bruised bits that sickened my
        spirit, licked my fingers clean, sneering,
      proud i attracted the king of beauty—
    was i...the queen? pride multiplied
my vertebrae, l o n g a n d l e a n
then i cursed all royalty who breathed.
envy cold-blooded me. he wasn't good
for me. but i couldn't leave. i'd think
    about another woman holding him.
      knowing him. having him. he was
        mine. mine. mine. my eyes became
          dichromatic, my body striped with
            red. greed took too much to name
            and i'd continue: the king of beauty
            was worth it. even when his eyes
            turned red. even when he hissed
        and shamed me. even when he
      rattled, pushed, constricted me
all wrath slithering out of his
throat: circle me, make me
scream, fang me, name me
venomous. I disassociated like
      it was hibernation, stagnated
        like a pool of murky water
          under a dried-up waterfall.
            then finally i thought
              speak! leave! but
              laziness forked
              my tongue and
              all that came
              out was a
              hiss.

THE NATURE OF IT ALL

The Pink Tax

blushed cheeks / dainty fingers / plucking flowers / turned into / pretty hair bows / pigtails / turned into / hot / pink polish / period pads / flirty shimmering lip gloss / turned into / sunset dates / plush blankets / blowing bubble gum / a boy's thirst for melons / areolas licked like whipped cream / cherry popping / tongue-tied stems / turned into / rose petal labia wilting / light bruising / cosmopolitans / strawberry daiquiris / galentine's day / turned into / sealed rouge lips / dainty fingers / blushed cheeks

what lies behind motive

beware, my friend, of righteous men
who claim to be and be to claim
for being requires no preaching
nor cares for monetary gain

beware, my friend, of friendly foe
who hate to love and love to hate
for darkness knows where darkness goes
and never reaps a prosperous fate

beware, my friend, of self-shadows
who choose ego and from ego choose
bulging heads walking blind through life
take paths that lead to aimless views

ponder, my friend, what humans intend
only truth ascends over ego in the end

THE NATURE OF IT ALL

The Disturbance

I wake mellow in a meadow
that's marshy and plush,
roll in the lush greenery, singing

lilac and lily lullabies,
harmonize with the river,
which is all toad and treasure.

Bang, there's a *bang* yelp *bang*
and a *bang* squeal *bang* in the
distance; and then, then silence—

heads hang heavy; a ripple
of sorrow gusts
through the grass like wind.

Oh, the shooters are blind,
are here to take the doe-
eyed. They want us, dear,

for food, fun, fame—dead. Still
I won't fear. I'll rest, then rear,
run until they disappear.

RYANNA HAMMOND

The Nature of It All

human
    animal

                    not so
                    different

on a destitute island
three million (chinstrap penguins) find refuge

the weary (lions) rest together in unruly
lands of drought, ribs poking out

the captive-bred (pandas) don't know
        gnashing teeth or demise of the weak

yet every animal knows
the nature of crooked (ego-filled humans)

some (foxes) lie in wait:
            opportunists

a frightened female (cheetah), saved, shivers in
a backseat, almost trafficked for the lust of her skin

the greedy kill the young (butterflies)
tack up their wings

in the darkest parts of earth
seven hundred (reef sharks) hunt
                              but just one eats

                                            the best photos show
                                            the worst moralities

THE NATURE OF IT ALL

Training

The same construction worker, Bill,
along with his team, come season after
season to work on Felton Street.

Each time he tells his workers
about what's happened underneath:
many trees' roots—silently beseeched—

went rampant and broke the pipes,
then the moistness of earth rallied and
wore the sewer and power lines.

The men nod in their hard hats, grab
the backhoes, jack hammers, shovels,
pound with purpose through the gravel.

The lines and pipes get reconfigured
with considerable will—it takes
fourteen grueling days until

the job is done, then Bill trains his son,
Bill Jr, to take over the company,
tells him he'll make very good money.

So season after season, year
after year, decade after decade,
Bill Jr trains, his Jr trains, and his

to do the same work, to fix
something that will never stay "fixed."
Earth continues; Earth rallies against.

RYANNA HAMMOND

From Flower to Stem

Together lying
in a luscious meadow

I: the flower,
He: the hand holding,
fingers plucking

slowly
one   by one   by one:

I love you

I love you not

I love you

I love you not

then I:
                    a
                 stem
begged him
to open his hand
and let me go.

dead roses

i wring the rose petals in the bathroom
sink. red dye drips down. flowers wilt. what
was i thinking? of course all flowers plucked
die, even these—no roots and too many
tears, water harvested for years in a clear
vase gone to waste. what more can i do?

the poor things are smooshed and bruised.
i yank on both the cold and hot, let all
the sustenance out. the sink bowl fills
as the petals swirl and whirl in circles
that get smaller, smaller, smaller, until
gone. swallowed by the welcoming drain.

i stare, unmoving, knowing i can't care
what's down there or where they'll go.

RYANNA HAMMOND

a shooting star shot out of the little dipper

little dipper love—you and i,
vast and wide, the only love
comparable to something

in the sky. i was all shine, but
never could you travel enough
light years to reach me. cold,

harsh atmosphere between   us.
was traditional love too much?
i looked across the cosmos to see

a couple intimately holding
hands, eyes locking in a way
ours never have, the man—

all smile—displays white roses,
"caroline, won't you be mine?
cheeks blush, she replies,

"only if you'll be mine." love
emanates as they kiss. finally i see
the big dipper sparkle in my periphery.

THE NATURE OF IT ALL

Depression

I'm alone on Thanksgiving and this
does not depress me. (Or does it?)
My mother called and asked

about the weather but I haven't felt it,
so I say it's nice. I'm sure it's nice.
Aren't most things? Eventually

I leave the house, walk to the park
I've been frequenting since childhood.
The ghost of seven-year-old me is

laughing, hanging on a tree branch.
Oh, she is happy. I wish I could be
a child here, even for just a moment,

feel what they feel, see what they see:
suddenly a small crow flies by with
an avocado in its mouth. I laugh,

and laugh, and laugh. Silly me thinking
only humans ate avocados. I imagine
myself as a bird, in a cozy nest, sharing

a meal, feeding babies, not thinking
too much, just being, just existing.
Then I count three hundred fall leaves

on a plain sycamore tree just to stop
my thoughts. And somehow
this all seems plain to me.

RYANNA HAMMOND

the human way

there was a blue house on hanover with three humans
and an olive tree in the front yard with generations and
generations of bees. even their ancestors were still there
in the dirt beneath the mailbox: a bee cemetery,

a few feet long, inches deep, thousands of decaying
carcasses heaped, all brittle thorax and partial grey wings.
often the bees moseyed over the graveyard like cars
slowing to a stop sign. they were visiting loved ones or

contemplating life as they stared at their inevitable fate:
old age, stepped on, releasing their stinger into someone,
too cold, too hot, caught in a web, human intrusion—
different routes with the same deafening end. oh the bees…

in summer heat they'd spread, fan their wings
across the blue popcorned wall by the front door;
in winter they'd huddle like a chunk of honey hanging
atop the porch light to stay warm. every morning

while working they'd bustle and swarm the yard.
by the time the sun sank a low hum could be heard
from the olive tree: they were curled asleep, and deep
inside was a mine of their golden homemade honey.

but then—they became hostile. two stung the child,
and the father was chased down the street. the following
morning, the mother was hounded by the tree. the family
gave in, summoned a beekeeper, thinking "what were we

supposed to do, other than safely remove the hive?"
their lawn had toted a sign: bee ware, bees live here.
as the mother yanked it from the dirt, she shed a tear;
they had all lived amicably, in harmony, for seven years.

Duality

two worlds
and i

belong to each

ego
stomps on

concrete - soul

vibrates
in realms

i cannot
see

i

stretch through
time, past the

concept of time,

where
there is

silence—

and it is

there
where

i am

no human, a speck
of light

Sacrifice

We live in a forest but forget
because it no longer looks
like a forest. There's too much:

houses, yards, plastic, toys,
trash, cash, balls, courts,
roads lined, and signs. *Caution:*

*There will be no stopping
any time soon.* Another breathless,
flattened squirrel is splayed

across the asphalt, blood and bone
everywhere, arms outstretched
and we need to ask ourselves:

whose sins did the squirrel die for?
I beg Nature to uncurl her vines, stretch
across the freeway, swallow it whole.

THE NATURE OF IT ALL

Wasteland

Her throat brimming
fury—the fuel for the fire.
It's natural, not

a disaster but a reaction
to the plastic
waste, the framework of her stomach.

She stopped releasing eons ago,
yet, she cries
from oil spills.

A cigarette hangs
out of mother
nature's mouth, tasting our bitter end.

Life Photography

Our eyes are cameras, capturing
the lens of our brains. Turn on
your flash, take these snaps:

Click: A baby duck can't
make the jump off a ledge—
its family continues to the river.

Click: Two stubborn people date:
love, wage wars, and swear
they're meant for each other.

Click: A young man lives a sober life
in Sin City, snubbing temptation
every time he leaves home.

Click: Best friends reside on opposite
sides of a country and the rate
of their phone calls slows.

From what angle are you looking?
How wide is your aperture?
Are the pictures light or dark?

THE NATURE OF IT ALL

?

this small world's one giant
unfolding of maybes; maybe

i'll spend a lifetime studying it.
maybe it's all right to think

us a glorified rodent, to laugh at
our ever-expanding teeth.

maybe at the core we are just
animal. maybe every species,

every atom, feels as much
as us. maybe this existence is

more than survival.
maybe we were an accident,

a brilliant one. maybe
we were planned, a sunbeam

turned tornado. maybe earth
will reclaim us as soil. maybe

i should just unwind, enjoy
the breathtaking sunrise.

CRACKS IN THE CONCRETE

THE NATURE OF IT ALL

golden grey morning

the alarm blares like the last bastard
in a bar on monday and i jolt awake,
just as i do every day. but today
i am welcomed by thick fog outside,
wonderfully curious. it slow dances
over the barely waking sky, hums through
this sparse forest, flirts with bright yellow
leaves on the neighbor's oak tree—

auspicious golden grey morning! it flaunts
itself like a honey-lipped woman in
a tight black dress. *hello, hello.* can i
stay in bed, watch you all morning? what if
i rise, slide the window open; won't you
come kiss me like you do the world?

awake(ning)

a world outside my window waits for me—
and yet   often i forget. i live a life
mercurial, confined: indoors and inside
my mind. i think i might be missing life.
i wake. i work. i stress. i sleep. repeat;
sometimes eat, maybe breathe, or believe

a world outside my window waits for me—
arms lining the ledge, i look longingly,
watching wild winds whisp among the leaves
of pepper trees confined like me, roots
restrained by concrete. yet, the winged ones
are free: the bumblebees, chevrons of geese.

a world outside my window waits for me—
i slide the glass ajar and feel the breeze.

THE NATURE OF IT ALL

the ants

i sit outside, chin to palms,
elbows to knees, watching
the vivacious ants march
their two-way highway.

they greet one another;
and one is lost, roaming
a few feet away; and another
attempts to reach the other

side of a trench: a crack
in the sidewalk. i lift my leg
and a third flees from under
my shoe. how confusing

that must have been—
going from day to night
to day in seconds. behind
a mountain: a rock, one

frantically carries his dead
comrade. i think to myself
i'm lucky, these ants all having
much crueler days than i.

RYANNA HAMMOND

a vortex

i was about to turn twenty-six when i first heard the term eddy:
water opposing the current that creates a whirlpool. as a verb, eddied

means to move in a circular way. swirl. spiral. whirl.
now, i think about eddies all the time. eddies

are always on my mind. i repeat, rehearse the definitions;
i want to see an eddy, to be eddied, to say eddy, eddy, eddy.

whenever i visit my hometown, i hope to find this specific
eddy whirring through my mind but that eddy

isn't on the freeway. at mcdonalds. mobil. in-n-out.
any stoplight. yes, i'm a silly girl. i hope to see an eddy

where an eddy probably won't be. it's always just a glance
that comes with the thought, "i wonder if i'll see an eddy

here." the last place i look: the freeway overlook. in my early twenties
i kissed the most memorable young man there. his name was——

i park, ask, "why here after nearly half a year?" no water this high,
not between my thighs nor in my eyes. see, i'm numb and dry. no eddy.

i lower the sunroof, listen to "I Was Made For Lovin' You." empty
passenger seat. it's just ryanna and chill air swirling in the breeze: an eddy,

but not the eddy i was hoping for.

THE NATURE OF IT ALL

survival

the bee, upside down
struggling,
spinning,
struggling

two furry black feet, tangled
inside a web spanning from
planter
 to wheelbarrow

the bee, upside down
twisting,
turning,
twisting

i collect the conniving
web, bring the bee
to safety—
one leg sticky, unmoving.

when the bee musters
strength to fly away,
i think about the spider,
now left hungry.

into midnight

pale baby
              blue skies all around
there's no escaping
              ineffable beauty on this
bluer-than-blue blue
              highway driving southbound

what can you do, but
              watch the orange setting sun
weep and bleed
              in the rearview with pastel hues—
by and by, a tangible ending
              another simple day

empty is met with empty when
              midnight is coming and
a heart is hollow—
              on tonight's forecast: swollen skies
filled with ceaseless rain
              fix your sight, just drive

chin up please, you can't yet see
              press the gas, welcome the changes
the unlimited future
              the effulgent full moon
hanging over
              the red-rocked mountains.

the cosmos, inducing your realignment—
              this is God's work:
happiness, gratitude, love,
              the spectrum of iridescent colors
and dreamy reveries
              that will never meet a permanent dusk.

THE NATURE OF IT ALL

a daily scavenger hunt for poems

       they get stuck between my teeth
and only a special toothpick can pull them
             out.

                some hang from the lemon tree
                in my childhood backyard
                and i'm still not tall enough
                    to reach them.

                                  they're always hiding in my car—
                                i find them when i'm roaming
                            from point a   to point b.

in Los Angeles i saw one in a woman swaying
   on a blanket on the corner of a busy street.
     she tilted her head back for her bottle
       and i watched it cascade down
         the fifth of vodka into her mouth.

                the other day i walked by two birds resting on a branch.
                    the first flew away but the other stayed
                      and sang me a poem of heartbreak.

       in the wind there's a plethora
        that gracefully fly and sometimes—
        with luck—i catch them, make them
          tangible.

                  i

                          find

                                            poems

    scattered—

                            everywhere
       i
             look.

Death Valley

It's fitting to visit a valley
of death alone after an ending:
empty road, quiet, barren
brown desert. There is so much

to notice in stillness—like the crow
flying by the car window:
a reminder that there is life beyond
the names of things. In the near distance,

there's voluminous layered mountains
growing, coating over
older selves with newer soils,
standing taller and changing hues

like the sky that warms the spirit,
wraps it with baby pinks and blues
in a blanket, like a child. Ah yes,
the sky is God and is everywhere.

There's no need to be scared of being
alone here—Death Valley is anything
but death. And a lone traveler is
anything but alone.

THE NATURE OF IT ALL

a soul waking up inside a human body

half-eaten apple in hand, sneakers pat
against pavement—this place
looks nothing like humanity's first days.
where did we go in "coming so far"?

the earth's sun sears a hellish heat
that seeps through pores, livens cells.
oh, the power of fruit and
light; i'm here inside a body.

i'm here inside a body!

hold out hands, expand
the spaces between fingers, feel
the sensation, notice
beyond the body: a backdrop—

a double-yellow-lined road, crows
cawing, clouds sauntering, an ancient
oak, a wheat-colored hill; everything
here is three dimensional.

everything here is three dimensional!

cheeks blush like ripe cherries, smile
beams pure, eyes become light rays—
aware of truth, awake, in one
blink: unleash heaven on earth.

trust the crisp sweetness like the birds.
this is a walking prayer. this realm:
a real lucid dream, a home to be,
and i won't die in permanent sleep.

i won't die in permanent sleep!

half marathon at dusk

adrenaline, adrenaline, a crowd,
a race commences—first step, build
momentum, focus on breath, in:
nose, out: mouth, steady, mile: two,

slow uphill, pace yourself, follow
the young fit man, weave through
the runners and desert sands, settle
in, crisp coolness on your skin, *see*

how the stars dance? mile: three,
see the sea of bobbing head lamps,
distant headlights? tender breeze
enrapture me! i'm alive, four, alive,

on a dirt-road-running-trail lined
with joshua trees on both sides,
five, senses heighten, runner's high
on life, *alive* alive, breath and feet

and heartbeat synchronize, don't think,
don't trip over feet, six, now sprint,
can you smell the half-way marker's
sweat? soaking from forehead to neck

to chest, pass the young man on the
left, focus on breath, seven, happy
tears surface the eyes, don't cry, don't,
eight, dry mouth, dry desert, parched,

water, ninth mile-marker, stop for
a second, sip electrolytes that dribble
down the chin, ten, happy tears again, like
a volcanic rupture, *let them leak,* eleven

walk if you need, almost done now,
almost—twelve, twitching, cramping,
keep sprinting, thirteen, tears flood
the eyes, dead yet alive, finish line.

Someone Has A Sweet Tooth

Look outside. Someone
blotted sunlight blush
across the mountainside,
blew their icy breath,
made mouth-watering
powdered sugar peaks.

Eons ago, Someone
must have hosted a feast
in the ether. The fallen
crumbs that came out
with divine laughter
fashioned grainy deserts.

Somewhere, Someone
is cooking the colors
of the sky—rainbow
sherbet, cotton candy
clouds—never mixing
the same sweetness twice.

Who served us such
a delectable earth?
Tell me, someone.

RYANNA HAMMOND

heaven on earth

paint this picture: you're on a desert highway
heading my way. there's a graffitied train
on your left, scattered clouds freshly fluffed
by angels, an orange glow from the setting
sun reflecting off your lashes. you're listening

to "whiskey woman" by flamin' groovies,
heading nowhere in particular, cruising
by semis, shrubbery, and powerlines,
nothing in particular on your mind,
and not a single dollar in your pocket.

here, now, you're seized by stillness.
trade this for any common scene: just be
a speck inside yourself—the body hollow,
yet filled with the zest of your youth—
and you will know   you have arrived.

THE NATURE OF IT ALL

her revival

in the meadows
the clouds had cried
while rivers froze
daffodils died
and winter arrived

...

the sun had gleamed
amidst the dew
while rivers streamed
daffodils grew
with spring anew

SOIL AND A THICKET

THE NATURE OF IT ALL

An Ode to North Carolina

I was a young ripe thing, just eighteen,
crying a river rugged enough to carry
my soul upstream through every memory
until I arrived on a twin bed in a small room
2,500 miles away from my childhood.

I learned to love Bojangles and Cook Out,
southern fast food chains with loads of sugar
in their sweet teas; to like new friends
with drawls, lengthy long distance calls, desolate
train tracks, a one-stop-light, Bible Belt town.

I found my lost self at chapel, in cold pews,
singing praise, arms raised, eyes closed, looking
for God, praying for a sermon to tell me why
good things have to change—no answers came—
too much to ask for an answer that lived in me.

I moved to the city: bar-hopping downtown,
fake friends at Ben's Tune Up, walking skinny
in a mini skirt, Off The Wagon Piano Bar, Jesus
was nowhere, smoking, drinking, weeping, doing
drugs, asking too many questions about love.

But then I began noticing—black bears roaming
before sunrise, thirty-degree sun-but-no-heat January
mornings, visible breath, falling leaves, Blue Ridge
Mountain me, four seasons equipped for change:
something that comes with no questions.

The Self Quest

through the windshield: ash-colored highway,
white lines and yellow lines that expand

forever in this finite moment. there is no end,
everywhere leads to somewhere leads to

somewhere else. i've found myself
on interconnected roads on the west coast,

heading to new places, adventures. however
even in new, the bloody truth always remains:

i can't run away from any part of me—
trauma, anxiety, hopes, dreams—

as i get closer to a future me who lives
righteously, anchored in the present, has

relinquished her fear of having fears. she
is why i long for long windy roads, for dull

desert terrain in one-hundred-degree heat or red
cartoon-like giant sequoia trees in green forests. she

is somewhere beyond this windshield, scattered
in fragments, across landscapes, behind boulders,

on mountain peaks, in silence—so i travel alone,
and piece more of her to my skin, my heart, my bones.

THE NATURE OF IT ALL

to live a quarter century

from listless abyss, i remember nothing as i went tumbling from the ether into flesh. at one, maybe peek-a-boo, only because i see myself in a baby's eyes—but the first core memory: death at age two, a crowd of people surrounding a casket that towered over me. three: death too, spinning in circles, laughing until a jolt of pain. my foot puffed red and i was sad the bee met its end. four: more dead. mommy turned the tv on frantically—we were holding hands; she was sad. on the screen: smoke, two towers. from the moment we're born we're living and dying all at once. a child has no time to notice—they're existing; my kindergarten teacher loved frogs like me and taught me this: *people say time flies when you're having fun, but frogs say times fun when you're having flies.* time wasn't flying so i must have been having flies, i thought: using disposable cameras in my room, capturing barbies and self-portraits with smacker's lip gloss. simple things like fake snow and hot cocoa made my day. i was an alien in the school play, won gold softball medals, had a father as a head coach, watched meteor showers in freezing weather, sang along to red hot chili peppers, and every summer there was family camping and beach days. the present moment was all i knew—then came: growing boobs, body hair, bullies. one girl treated me like i was something disposable—didn't recycle me into the sea of seventh graders but decomposed me. i put on a smile mask, created red and white flesh zebra-striped arms, and picked myself apart like i was a shitty piece of abstract art. i no longer cared about fun or flies, only death—we return to what we know and there's a spiritual sickness across the globe. if i am a snail, ego deshelled me. i tumbled away from this skin, became nothing more than an island far out in the sea. not a single soul could reach me. then religion pricked my finger and immediately gave me a band-aid, so i sat down on christianity's couch and prayed to protect my holy virginity. until the bottle came along and gave me even more praise, the price: inhibition. i loved users and abusers—gave them so much more than my virginity—and life was a party: blurry vision, brain cell collision. Then a drunk skeleton tumbled, by god's grace, into therapy, wrote poetry, drank hot tea, went hiking—meditated over medicated, i now dance and dance to my own soundtrack, its volume only getting louder and more attuned.

finally grounded
in skin, i know why i am:
live in love in flesh.

q & a with my most peaceful self

what does tomorrow hold?
today

why am i here?
you are

am i following the right path?
you are on your path

what should i focus on?
being

will you stay with me?
i am

why do i hold so much fear?
because you haven't let it go

THE NATURE OF IT ALL

A Desert Sunset

An ocean of strawberry lemon clouds
barrels into swirly snowcapped peaks.

Fresh desert air hums between
immeasurable Joshua trees.

Even the plain brown grains are
holy. Oh, cast your sight quickly!

Blackness has been waiting to hum
melodies with wind, to tuck us in.

God gifted all of us this: unleashed
pure beauty from heaven, spilled

it onto earth, let it run
amok—just to see us

look up
and smile.

Oh to be like Rock purslane

their flimsy sea green stem bodies stretch
three feet high into the sky,

sway in support of their intense
open-faced magenta flower heads

that look up, up, into light rays
living in a constant state of praise.

THE NATURE OF IT ALL

My God Is

As a child I saw a man
who lived in the sky.
I was never sure where but
                                    somewhere,
                                                              above the clouds.

He was scary, grey,
made of cloud, thunder, rain,
pointing a lightning finger
at humans—only some were His
chosen ones so He killed people.
He forced them to sacrifice their
sons, lovers, babies, homes—Oh,
spiteful eye condemning from the sky!

God, i hated the word God! I hated
the angle of the picture that was taken
and handed to me from the blurry lens of
        imperfect humans who passed down
        imperfect stories with
        imperfect ideologies and
        imperfect agendas full of the
        imperfect idea that
to love is to fear
when really
       to love is
               to love is
                      to love is
                             to love.

                                       And to love
is to humble, know
humility, and, by God,
the ego of humanity is not
principal, nor will it ever be!

You know, I've always known
there existed a power greater
than me, but from the snapshot I got
I didn't know how to see—until
one day I was running in
the mountains and the wind

whispered to me. Peace
rushed over me and through me
and chills crept up my spine.
I didn't know
what to call it
so I called it

God

G – O – D

Greatness Of Divinity:

the expanse, something sacred
that I can't quite define because
that which cannot fit into a box
will never be forced into one!

My God is as thin as air,
adaptable to squeeze
into every atom of existence.

My God is here
now,
                         and there
                              now,
and was here
before,

                                                         and will be here
                                                               later.

My God doesn't live in

                                              the sky,

my God lives everywhere, including
where you are.

My God is the light itself
and can be found
in light and in light's absence.

My God is a silent whisper
and a silent whisperer.

THE NATURE OF IT ALL

My God is a child's laughter.

My God is an ancient
oak, a river, and the smallest
rock inside of it.

My God is a single thump of a heartbeat.

                                          My God is inside every poem
                                              if you look close enough.

My God is not a building, not a book
but can be found in one.

My God is in every religion
and no religion, is not a religious
war and will never be found
                              in one.

My God has no gender and yet
is found in every gender, goes by many
names and sometimes has no name at all.

My God is,
exists.

                                                    My God is here
                                                      now.

                    My God may not be
                  your God and your God
                    may not be   my God
            (or you may not have a God) and
                my God! I love you anyway!

I Am

soul—rain on a rainy day, sun on a sunny day

a holy painting baptized in watercolors from the Creator's paintbrush

a creation that has the ability to create

a pinky promise between Consciousness and Love

wedded to Growth—life's experiences conjure the ring to my finger

an ant—beady eyes looking to endless skies

too much for those who only seek little

royalty birthed

from the belly of heartbreak, fixing my crown until it firmly fits

nothing, everything; a moment, an eternity; a void, a universe

THE NATURE OF IT ALL

At The Center

I will not deny myself
                the pleasure of being
a dichotomy, of reshaping
                the plastic mold society
has designed for me. I'm tired
                of watching the pendulum
swing, each day accepting
                only parts of me.
Swing.
            Swing.
    Swing.
                Swing.
    All that left-and-right makes me
        dizzy. I am a rap song about pussy
and a gospel hymn praising
            the highest entity. I am
a short pink schoolgirl skirt,
            a teacher's blue blouse,
an afternoon hike in a pine forest,
        and a night out, roaming city streets.
I am sobriety and CBD-infused tea,
            not afraid of what earth
        provides for me. I am deep-
            fried chicken and a low sugar
        oat milk ice cream. I'm a tomboy
            some nights, and others I'm your
        girly girl dream. I am spiritual
            and I cuss a lot. And, suddenly,
        my pendulum has stopped—
        at the center there's only
        the slightest sway.

RYANNA HAMMOND

My World

I once made my world so, so
small it was the size of one blue man. The only
color I saw was the pigment of his skin. I saw nothing
when I looked into his eyes. Time and time again, my spirit
nearly died—too dim—from trying to pin Love like a tail onto
him. Blinded, I missed, and missed, and missed, because Love is
too grand to be placed on a man—a lesson learned over heartbreaks
that caused my world to expand, expand, expand, and the other day
I bought a plastic slice of pizza from my niece for an invisible sixty-eight
dollars. My father celebrated sobriety in the three-digit numbers, and
the majority of the population knows nothing of the strength and grace
that takes. It still stuns me that my sister goes by the name "Mommy."
I've learned I'm allowed to masturbate and praise the divine power of my
pussy. On long drives I watch clouds become God. On special occasions
I microdose on shrooms and run half marathons. My younger cousin is
navigating her early twenties, and I watch her bloom like a summer lily.
"Goodnight, Baby," I say to my nephew as we curl in for the night.
Eight hours later I wake to his eager ocean eyes, buzzed blonde
hair, soft sweet smile, like heaven staring at me. He whispers,
"Good Morning, Auntie" and I reply, "Good Morning,
Baby," as warmth radiates through me, eliminating
the last traces of blue in my being. And now
my sublime world is so vast
it requires a map—
and everything in it is painted in yellow, light rays and endless
dawn, always, always, and again becoming. And all of it is
Love—even without a lover.

THE NATURE OF IT ALL

circles

there's reason
why

pi
has no end

all
circles extend

through
forever's ever

on this spinning
sphere;

here
all mothers

bore mothers
who bore more mothers

life's cycle—
light

helps soil
helps grass

helps grasshoppers,
helps snakes,

helps a hardy hawk in the sky
that eventually dies,

decays,
its body

reclaimed
by fungi who take

the feathered body
and make

RYANNA HAMMOND

mineral salt that
goes back

to the grass
for life

to continue 'round
and 'round and 'round

THE NATURE OF IT ALL

An Infinite Constant

Mother, like God,
is forever

something
I can't define—

a bottle of Jesus-
made wine,

the bottomless
nectar of life,

on the surface
of heaven.

Family Weddings

Intently we watch, heads cocked.
The bride appears, beautiful
as ever. The groom smiles a smile
I've never seen—one that'll be
sore by the end of the evening.

Vows are woven with a kiss into
the night air. Angels hover over
their son's wedding, alongside
ancestors, stars—if you quiet,
their cheering can be heard.

Bellies are filled with wine and
the dance floor is filled with
parents, siblings, aunts, uncles,
cousins, cousin's cousins. Some
faces have aged fifteen years

since I've seen them. What's more:
a few have passed, a few arrived.
Like a prayer we recite, "We must
see each other more often." Truly,
we must. I'm all smile, beaming,

then I spill on my dress. Upset,
I tell the child on my left. She
says it's okay; she's spilled, too.
Her once cream-colored dress is
adorned with both dirt and juice.

Jovial, she scampers off to play
with others in the grass and I laugh.
She nonchalantly holds the secret
to a happy life at her fingertips:
surface stains are no match for Love.

THE NATURE OF IT ALL

Age With Grace

I used to think the phrase "Age with grace"
was talking about physical beauty.

Minimize stress to minimize wrinkles.

Avoid the sun so you won't develop dark spots.

I thought it was something for old people
to help them look young.

Age with grace.

As I've gotten older—grown closer to God,
shook Grace's hand time and time again—
the phrase has taken on a new meaning.

Don't be a lemon when you can be a berry.

Don't let your hardships turn you into a stone wall.

Don't judge others for the parts of yourself that you don't like.

Age with grace.

Realize that nobody knows what they're doing,
including you.

Mentor and support the generation coming after you.
As they collect the fruit of life,
give them a reusable grocery bag.

Age with grace.

It does have something to do with beauty—
beauty from the inside rather than the outside.

Toddlers and Their Why

Oh, the toddlers are so new and curious,
running amok, blabbering gibberish, and jumping
off rocks to feed the daredevil inside,
asking adults "why" about everything in life.

We need to walk instead of run down the hill. Why?
Please be careful by the fire. Why?
We're going to roll up the window on the highway. Why?
You can't have any more sweets right now. Why?

And with each adult answer—whether easy to gather
or crafted in the moment—comes a quizzical look
followed by another "Why?" The toddler questions
our answer, which makes us stop to rethink life.

Why don't we eat the leaf on top of the strawberry?
Why is the wood of the fire making a snapping sound?
Why do we not talk to strangers?
Why is it not dessert before dinner?

Why don't we have more questions?
Why do we always have answers?
Why do we lose the curiosity of the toddler
when this world becomes familiar?

THE NATURE OF IT ALL

A Gift

For Jayd Lynne

God sat down with a group of souls, said
"The next one going to Earth is special."
Their birthday: Valentine's. The day of
universal love. A soul selfless in flesh
was needed—who'd give flowers and gifts
on a day when they were meant to receive,
who had a heart so magnanimous
it barely fit in their chest. Every soul
volunteered, and you were sitting patiently.
God held out a hand and said, "You."

RYANNA HAMMOND

two bound to touch in carlsbad, new mexico

seventy-five stories below, we strolled
together through a vast dimly lit cavern,
reacquainting. it had been six years since
we'd been college friends. we learned

limestone walls are complex, made of
many substances; when matter decays,
new interconnections are made. we glanced
at each other, marveled at the odd-

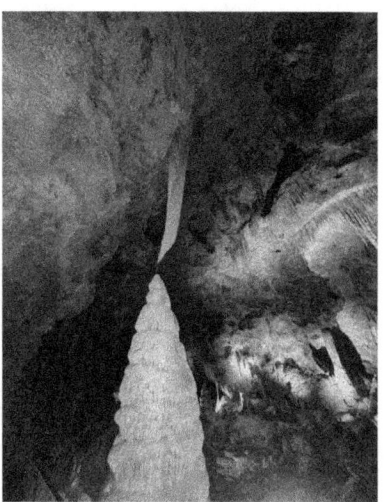

shaped speleothems, how things that seem
lifeless can grow. icicle-shaped stalactites
hung from the ceiling; mountain-shaped
stalagmites grew up from the floor. each

began the same way: with a mineral-
filled drop of water. we were curious,
asking: are they hollow? well-rounded?
growing? not concerned with surface facts

like color, height, or shape? it was touching
how some icicles and mountains became one.
miles in we found a pair close to acquainting,
just five inches between them. in water droplets

that's the distance from atlanta to los angeles.
they were aligned—the same water sustenance
feeding them both, drawing them close. we
calculated how long it would take them to meet:

dependent on rainfall and heat, they'd touch
in 41 years and 8 months, which seemed
far but we didn't lose heart. for a cavern
half a megayear, that's only a bat of an eye.

THE NATURE OF IT ALL

Where Love Is Loudest

I'd just wiped my last tears
with dirt in an empty flower bed
filled with bittersweet memories
when I took off my shoes

and danced alone in the grass
with the trees and winds,
paying no mind to the things
trying to capture my time—

men on broken unicycles and
clowns juggling sex and bottles.
I made tenderness from hands,
then birthed heaven's bliss

from within—and that's when
I heard it: the thump of a wild
beating heart. Across the grass,
on the other side of the park,

was a young man full of life—
beaming smile, colored cheeks,
a soft aura containing a child's
"cheese" and gentleman's "please."

He was sitting on a picnic blanket
alone, among abundance: limes,
sobering wines, and plates and
plates of ripe berries and grapes.

My heart beat like his—signals.
Our eyes met and I knew better
than to walk—worthy and winged,
I flew to where love was loudest.

physical touch: a language

shut eyes, silent mouths, and still
there's speaking in two intertwining

hands: *we're in this together*, the
caress against an arm: *i'm here*,

palms framing a face: *do you see
i'm locked in*, meeting cheek to cheek:

i seek to share the same air, soft
pecks: *we are real*, a hug becomes more

snug: *come nearer*, a spine-trail of kisses:
i love how you carry yourself, cariño

in bed, skin stroking skin, a hymn:
feel me, feel me, feel me again, the dance—

souls braiding through love-making:
we were two and now we're one.

THE NATURE OF IT ALL

The Earth Band

Who does the Earth play for?
Hush—if we're quiet, we'll hear it.
Three, two, one, it's *The Daily Song*:
Bees hum, reverberation of a drum!

Hush, hush your mind, you'll hear it.
Crickets, cicadas, grasshoppers, gather with
Bees: hum like the reverberation of
a drum! Who can rattle like a maraca?

Crickets, cicadas, grasshoppers, trill and chirp!
Humans, do you hear it? Join the laughter!
Snake, that rattle's a sensational beat!
Mammals—join in! Howl, cry, sing.

Humans, do you hear it? Join with laughter!
This orchestra has an invisible conductor.
Mammals—join in! Howl, cry, sing.
Someone is cheering, beaming.

This orchestra has an invisible conductor.
There's an instrument for all—*The Daily Song*:
Someone is cheering, beaming.
Who? Who does Earth play for?

One Big Jam Session

life force
on the drums
creating a rhythm
a deep thump

ta ta ta

on the triangle
between gut and
head and heart
intuition starts

ting ting ting

i hear the music
and know i'm
on the cusp
of something

soul's purpose
gets on guitar
and confidently
strums the strings

du nuh nuh nuh nuh

my human experience
steps to the mic
and starts to sing
to the jovial beat

instinctively my feet
stomp and my body
bops, aligned with
tempo and time

du nuh nuh nuh nuh
ta ting ta ting ta ting

THE NATURE OF IT ALL

the heavens
and angels
are backstage
cheering

they shine lights,
beyond bright,
for me to truly see
everyone's lovely faces

du nuh nuh nuh nuh
ta ting ta ting ta ting

i look out and see
god
god
god

OTHER WORKS

Excerpt from *We Are Human*

longing

she longs for a lover—
one who values
her mind more than her body.
one who cherishes
every thought, feeling, emotion—
as if they were articles of clothing,
delicate and revealing.
one who finds beauty
in her naked mind
as she exposes them to rawness
that others shall never see.
one who would rather
undress her mind
before undressing her clothes.

Excerpt from *Hearts Bruise Never Break*

obliteration

there is a hollow room in my mind. the label on the door reads "you." i'm welcomed in by cobwebs and darkness. my memories are all that are left here, playing like a scratchy VHS tape. there are good ones. sour ones. random ones. the ones i wish i could forget. it has been a while since i've been here. i replay our memories. rewind, play, pause. rewind, play, pause. somehow i'm always surprised to see that our story ends in the exact same way. the same painful way.

-i'm cutting the videotape.

Excerpt from *My Cup of Coffee*

if i am what i enjoy

if i am
what i enjoy
then i am
a steaming cup of coffee
at six in the morning,
a solo dance
to meditation music,
a stroll through the park
as dusk is approaching,
my boyfriend's soft grey sweater,
a choir in unison,
snuggles under warm blankets,
my dog's smile,
christmas lights
in the middle of july,
the smell of a campfire,
frogs croaking by the creek,
anything chocolate,
and the puffy clouds
rolling in over the mountains.

if i am
what i enjoy
then
i truly love myself.

Excerpt from *The Door Between Us*

the first dance

i took my own hand,
asked myself to dance.
between us we had three left feet
and one right.
we s t umbled
stumb l e d
stumbled
before i dipped myself
in a backbend so low
i almost broke,
snapped myself in two.
but with the strength of my core
i lifted myself proudly above my head.
after landing the pose
i extended my hand
to myself with confidence.
we continued the dance
twirling
        twirling
twirling
        in circles
through the city streets.
i looked in my eyes with admiration,
then presented myself with a rose
realizing this woman standing before me
was everything
and i vowed to myself
i would always be
the best dance partner.

Excerpt from *Skinny Dipping with Patience*

deep-rooted

if you want to learn of love
that lasts a lifetime, look
to the pair of joshua trees
careening in the barren desert.

forever frozen
in a ballroom dance:
he dips her low, grips her trunk
with his burliest branch.

these conjugal trees,
once mere seeds, together
grew at analogous speeds,
sharing scarce water beneath

the earth's surface
where their roots are entwined—
they will live a life together
and, at some point, together die.

Excerpt from *Searching For Emiliano*

PROLOGUE

It's curious how people can live in the same town nearly their entire lives and yet their paths will never cross. As one exits the parking lot, the other has just parked. As one orders an ice cream cone, the other walks out of the shop looking down at their phone. As one goes from aisle five to aisle six examining their grocery list, the other brushes past them into aisle five.

And this truth is no different for the residents of Old Oak, California; what with its nearly 40,000 residents any two people could be under each other's noses quite often and one or both of them may never know it.

One person who never notices such things is Rachel Williams. She tends to be aloof, a bit in the clouds. Not in the way of an idiot, but in the way of an overthinker. Everywhere she goes, her body is in reality, but her mind is somewhere else. And that's why she never notices people.

As it turns out though, people notice her. They have an affinity for her upbeat spirit and intellect. She's got the kind of personality that Curiosity wants to taste, that Misery wants to tarnish, that Pain wants to kill. On top of her character, she's got an athletic physique that turns heads and a natural beauty that shines with or without makeup.

One such person who has always been drawn to Rachel is Javier Aguilar. He grew up just four blocks away from her, and prior to her moving away for college, he would see her all the time. They went to the same elementary school, and that's where he first saw her. She was in third grade, he in sixth. And, unfortunately for him, their age gap meant they would never be in middle school together. By the time he was off to high school, the boundaries within the city limits that designated which school one would attend changed. Rich neighborhoods were popping up just over the hill, so the cutoff line became the main road between his house and Rachel's. She went to Old Oak High School and he went to Ten Pines High School, the next town over.

Now, he is twenty-six and she twenty-three, and he is still trying to meet her. However, outside of the elementary school setting, their near run-ins were never by accident. Javier wanted to run into Rachel, and often sought her out. In middle school, he would walk by her house every morning on the way hoping to meet her. In high school, he would try to hang around the same crowd as her or go to her soccer matches, hoping to enter her circle. Some might think that to be embarrassing or ridiculous, others may believe it to be charming. He stopped trying when she moved away to college over half a decade ago and set his sights elsewhere. He has no idea that she has been back for a year.

Another such man who has had near run-ins with Rachel is Emiliano Morales. However, unlike Javier, his near run-ins with her were never planned; rather, they were coincidence, random, accidental. He went to middle school and high school with Rachel and would often pass by her in the hallways, see her playing in her high school soccer games, or spot her occasionally at a party.

In the grand scheme of school life however, it wasn't truly that often. They were from completely different crowds, cultures, and lifestyles. Unlike Rachel or Javier who belong to the dominant American culture and live in middle class neighborhoods, Emiliano is heavily immersed in his Mexican heritage and is first generation in the United States.

Growing up, his family often relocated from one rented room to another, until he turned fifteen and a half and was able to get a job. By that point, with his sister being seventeen, they both worked. And—finally—he, his mother, and his sister, were able to afford their own condo with the help of an undocumented immigrant and her son who paid rent to them under the table for one bedroom. From the time he was sixteen to now, age twenty-two, his immediate family has lived in that same condo, in one of Old Oak's few barrios, which is nestled between the 101 freeway and the town's only true *Mexicano* shops.

His life has been filled with hustle, grind, and labor for as long as he can remember to help his family survive. So, no, he hasn't thought about Rachel since high school, and truly he rarely thought about her then. He had no breaths or seconds to waste thinking about the beautiful Rachel Williams from an entirely different world who didn't even know he existed. She was merely a pretty White girl with privileges he could only dream of. It wouldn't matter to him whether or not she is back home from college or that she even left for college in the first place.

However, on this oddly serendipitous October morning, Rachel Williams, Javier Aguilar, and Emiliano Morales have all planned to attend the same pickup soccer game at a park in Old Oak. In just two hours' time, all three of their paths will cross—the match that, when lit, will spark inevitable change in each of their lives forever.

Notes

Seven Deadly Serpents first appeared in *(w)holes: An Anthology from the Heartland Society of Women Writers*.

The Nature of It All is an ekphrastic poem, meaning it was crafted based on another work of art. Each scene in the poem is describing a famous photo from National Geographic's *100 Best Photos* Magazine. The poem speaks the loudest when it is read in two ways: first with the parenthetical remarks, second without the parenthetical remarks.

Training and *Sacrifice* first appeared on the radio show *Environmental Directions* hosted by Nancy Pearlman on KBPK 90.1 FM.

My World first appeared in *dialogue: reflection* literary magazine by Empower Her* Voice.

A handful of poems from this collection were originally brought to poetry workshop classes at Emerson College from 2021 through 2024 when I was obtaining my MFA degree. They would not present so beautifully if it weren't for all the helpful feedback from my professors and peers.

I use quite a few poetry forms in this book. I often don't think it important to note or mention which form was used, however in the case of *into midnight* I do. This poem is known as a contrapuntal, which is technically multiple poems in one. You can read the left column alone, the right column alone, and both columns together (the standard way: from left to right, down the page).

Acknowledgments

Thank you to my mother for always listening to my poems and being my biggest supporter.

Thank you to my father for always providing me with a solid foundation and home; two things vital for growth in any aspect of life.

Thank you to the love of my life, WaVE Carranza, for being my best friend and the biggest supporter of my work (alongside my mom).

Thank you to every teacher I have had from kindergarten through my MFA classes. I wouldn't be a writer if it weren't for each of you.

Thank you to Mother Earth for guiding me to Peace and Truth.

Thank you to Love, the highest essence, for pointing the way on this human journey.

About the Author

Ryanna Hammond is a human being, who is probably "being" just like you—with unique quirks, flaws, passions, and unanswered questions. She writes with the aim to connect with others and help them feel less alone in this peculiar thing called human existence at this peculiar time in history. She has a BA in Psychology (2019) from UNC Asheville and an MFA in Creative Writing with an emphasis in poetry from Emerson College (2024). This is her sixth poetry collection.

Instagram: @soulledwanderess
TikTok: @soulledwanderess

About the Publisher

All With Heart is more than just a publisher; it is a podcast, a brand, and a lifestyle founded by Ryanna Hammond. As a human she aims to live her life all with heart—AKA be vulnerable, help the human species expand, share her passions, learn from others, be a student of life, and ultimately live a wild, free, and bold life with her heart wide open. She hopes that All With Heart—through books, services, merch, events, and more—will inspire others to do the same.

Instagram: @itsallwithheart
TikTok: @itsallwithheart

Index

?, 32
a compilation of excuses, 16
a daily scavenger hunt for poems, 40
A Desert Sunset, 52
A Gift, 66
a shooting star shot out of the little dipper, 25
a soul waking up inside a human body, 42
a vortex, 37
Age With Grace, 64
An Ode to North Carolina, 48
An Infinite Constant, 62
At The Center, 58
awake(ning), 35
circles, 60
dead roses, 24
Death Valley, 41
deep-rooted, 78
Depression, 26
Duality, 28
Family Weddings, 63
From Flower to Stem, 23
golden grey morning, 34
half marathon at dusk, 43
heaven on earth, 45
her revival, 46
I Am, 57
if i am what i enjoy, 76
into midnight, 39
Life Photography, 31
longing, 74
My God Is, 54
My World, 59
obliteration, 75
Oh to be like Rock purslane, 53
One Big Jam Session, 71
physical touch: a language, 69
q & a with my most peaceful self, 51
Sacrifice, 29
Searching For Emiliano Prologue, 79
Seven Deadly Serpents, 17
Someone Has A Sweet Tooth, 44
survival, 38
the ants, 36
The Disturbance, 20
The Earth Band, 70
the first dance, 77

the human way, 27
The Nature of It All, 21
The Pink Tax, 18
The Self Quest, 49
to live a quarter century, 50
Toddlers and Their Why, 65
Training, 22
two bounds to touch in carlsbad, new mexico, 67
Wasteland, 30
what lies behind motive, 19
Where Love Is Loudest, 68

www.ingramcontent.com/pod-product-compliance
Lightning Source LLC
Chambersburg PA
CBHW020557030426
42337CB00013B/1126